D1116334

SEISMOSAURUS

SAURUS

The Longest Dinosaur

by Don Lessem

illustrations by Donna Braginetz

 Carolrhoda Books Inc./Minneapolis

Carolrhoda Books, Inc. c/o The Lerner Group
241 First Avenue North, Minneapolis, MN 55401

Library of Congress Cataloging-in-Publication Data

Lessem, Don.
    Seismosaurus : the longest dinosaur / by Don Lessem
; illustrations
by Donna Braginetz.
        p. cm.
    Includes index.
    Summary: Describes the research and paleontological
investigation that led to the identification and classifica-
tion of the dinosaur Seismosaurus.
    ISBN 0-87614-987-5
    1. Seismosaurus—Juvenile Literature. [1.
Seismosaurus.
    2. Dinosaurs.] I. Braginetz, Donna. II. Title.
QE862.S3L4685   1996
567.9'7—dc20   95-36473
                                              CIP
                                              AC

Manufactured in the United States of America
1 2 3 4 5 6 – JR – 01 00 99 98 97 96

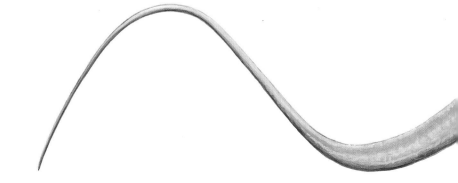

To Paula Apsell, a friend, and a friend of science—D.L.
To Mom and Dad—D.B.

The morning is quiet along the shores of a shallow blue lake in what is now New Mexico, 145 million years ago. Plant-eating, or **herbivorous,** dinosaurs of many sizes and shapes roam along the shore, nibbling at greenery. The biggest plant-eaters are as long as houses and as tall as office buildings, and they lumber along on four stout legs.

Suddenly the morning hush is broken by a peculiar rumbling sound. The ground vibrates louder and louder beneath the feet of the dinosaurs. Puddles of water shake, and the muddy shore quakes.

The thudding sound grows deafening. Over a rise a huge leg appears, and then another. As they land, the monster's feet splatter the muddy lakeshore. As they rise, a loud sucking sound pops in the ears of other fleeing dinosaurs. Looking back as they run in its long shadow, the dinosaurs see a creature about four school buses long.

Meet the longest animal ever to walk the Earth—*Seismosaurus,* the "Earth-shaker reptile."

A model of *Tyrannosaurus rex*. *T. rex* is famous for its size, but it wasn't the largest dinosaur that ever lived.

One of the most fascinating and awe-inspiring features of dinosaurs is their size. But not all dinosaurs were giants. Most were no bigger than a car, and some were as small as chickens.

Still, some dinosaurs did indeed grow huge, huger than any living thing before or since on land. We love to think about record-setters, especially with dinosaurs—which was the biggest, the meanest, the strongest, the fastest? When it comes to figuring out which was the biggest of all dinosaurs, the question itself needs careful definition.

What do we mean by the biggest? Do we mean the tallest? Or the heaviest? Or the longest? Deciding which is the tallest dinosaur is difficult, since dinosaurs didn't stand tall like we do. Most stood with their tails raised and their heads lowered. Their posture was more horizontal than vertical.

How about the heaviest dinosaur? Well, we don't know how heavy any dinosaur was. Sometimes if we're lucky, we can find almost the complete skeleton of a dinosaur. In the many years of searching for dinosaurs, scientists have found only about 2,100 such skeletons, and few of these come from the biggest dinosaurs.

Allosaurus, like most dinosaurs, stood with its head lowered and its tail raised.

A *Brachiosaurus* skeleton, and two versions of what the living dinosaur might have looked like, depending on its weight

Even if we have all of a dinosaur's bones, though, we don't have the organs that went inside them, or the flesh and muscles that contributed to the dinosaur's total weight. So it's very difficult to guess the exact weight of a dinosaur. We know the biggest dinosaurs weighed many tons, but just how many, whether 50 tons or 100 tons or more, isn't certain. We can look at the relationship of bones to body weight in living animals. Then, based on the size of a dinosaur's bones and the size of impressions made in bones by muscles, we can make some guesses about what the dinosaur might have weighed. But some dinosaurs, especially the meat eaters, had bones with more holes in them than others did. So we have no way of knowing how accurate our guesses about dinosaur weight might be.

Perhaps the most answerable of all questions about giant dinosaur size is "Which dinosaur was the longest?" That's a question that doesn't depend on guessing how a dinosaur stood, or what its missing parts weighed. The length of an animal matches well to the length of its skeleton, and if you have its skeleton, you can easily measure how long it was, head to toe. Even if you don't have the whole skeleton, you can often estimate, from the part you do have, how long that animal probably was. But as you'll see, "Which dinosaur was the longest?" is still not an easy question to answer for certain. Not all giant dinosaurs were built alike. Comparing a small part of one dinosaur to the skeleton of another may not be an accurate way to estimate the size of the newfound fossil animal.

By comparing this *Acrocanthosaurus* skull to the skulls of other dinosaurs, scientists can make guesses about the creature's overall size.

Although *Allosaurus* (above) was a large dinosaur, some of the plant-eating dinosaurs that lived at the same time were much larger.

In most environments, past and present, the very largest animals have been plant-eaters, whether elephants in the African savanna, moose in the Maine woods, or plant-eating dinosaurs in the world of 145 million years ago.

Perhaps some plant-eaters grow so large because they don't have to be swift-moving to find food, as many meat-eaters, or **carnivores,** do. Or maybe the great size of plant-eaters is itself a defense against attack. Whatever the reason, plant-eating dinosaurs grew more than twice the length, and probably many times the weight, of the longest **predators,** or hunters, of their world, such as the 20- to 45-foot long *Allosaurus*.

All of the longest known dinosaurs belong to one group of plant-eaters, the **sauropods.** These herbivores had small heads and big bellies. They walked on four legs and had long necks and tails.

Scientists have named and identified more species, or kinds, of sauropods than any other types of dinosaurs. **Paleontologists,** the scientists who study **fossils,** have grouped these dinosaurs into many smaller categories called subgroups, according to their different shapes.

A skeleton of the large sauropod *Apatosaurus,* which was about 70 feet long and may have weighed close to 25 tons

13

The sauropods in the **brachiosaur** sub-group, such as *Brachiosaurus* and *Ultrasaurus,* had longer front limbs than back limbs and had high chests like giraffes. They are best known from the end of the **Jurassic** Period, 145 million years ago, in both western North America and East Africa. They seem to have been built for feeding high in the trees and may even have reached to the tops of the trees by rearing up on their hind legs. They may have been the heaviest of all dinosaurs, if we guess by the size of their huge, thick limbs. They were long indeed, some more than 80 feet in length. Scientists found the first brachiosaur fossils in North America in the late 1800s.

Brachiosaurs may have been the ancestors of another major group of sauropods, the **titanosaurs.** These dinosaurs had longer back legs than front legs, unlike brachiosaurs. And their necks were shorter than those of brachiosaurs. They were huge, however, growing as long and as wide as the biggest brachiosaurs.

In the Southern Hemisphere, titanosaurs dominated the last dinosaur period, the **Cretaceous** (144 million to 65 million years ago). They were not present at all in North America until the very end of dinosaur time. But in South America, they reached huge sizes. The recently-named titanosaur *Argentinosaurus* may have been the heaviest of all dinosaurs, judging by the size of its huge **vertebrae,** or backbones, each five feet high and wide. Though fewer than one-third of this dinosaur's bones have been found, scientists estimate it may have measured 115 feet long. *Argentinosaurus* lived about 90 million years ago.

Other huge titanosaurs, some with armored sides, lived right to the end of dinosaur time, 65 million years ago. While not as huge as *Argentinosaurus,* they were all giants.

Saltasaurus (above) was small for a titanosaur—only about 40 feet long—but its body armor must have helped protect it from attackers.

Camarasaurus (above) and its relatives were shorter sauropods than the diplodocids, but they may have weighed more.

Scientists also discovered another group of giant sauropods in the American West nearly a century ago. These giants lived at the same time as the brachiosaurs, 145 million years ago. They were the **diplodocids.** Their bones were narrower than those of the brachiosaurs and titanosaurs, and so they were more lightly built than those other sauropods. But they were longer than the brachiosaurs, with long, whiplike tails. Some diplodocids, like *Apatosaurus* (formerly known as *Brontosaurus*) and *Diplodocus,* grew to nearly 100 feet long.

Apatosaurus (left) and *Diplodocus*

The largest complete dinosaur skeleton was made from fossils of several animals discovered nearly 100 years ago. It belongs to a dinosaur named *Brachiosaurus*. The skeleton of this enormous creature came not from western North America but from what is now Tanzania, in eastern Africa. German scientists discovered the skeleton early in the 20th century. Hundreds of porters carried the bones to the sea. The bones were then shipped back to Germany for cleaning and putting back together. The brachiosaur was mounted in a museum in Berlin, Germany, where it still stands, 82 feet long and nearly 40 feet high. *Diplodocus* fossils have been mounted in an even longer skeleton, 89 feet long.

Below: Part of a long *Diplodocus* backbone found at Dinosaur National Monument in the southwestern United States. *Opposite page:* A complete *Brachiosaurus* skeleton

It was not until the 1970s that another strong claim was made to the title of the longest dinosaur. "Dinosaur Jim" Jensen was a former dock worker in Alaska and a mechanic for the paleontology department at Harvard University. Although he didn't have much formal education, Dinosaur Jim had a lot of energy and a great love for dinosaurs. Eventually he found a job digging up dinosaur fossils for Brigham Young University in his native Utah. In 1972, on a coffee table in the home of an amateur fossil collector in western Colorado, Jensen saw an enormous leg bone that was shaped like the leg bones of typical meat-eating dinosaurs. Jensen asked the collector, Eddie Jones, to show him where the bone had been found.

Jones took Jensen to the windy highlands of Dry Mesa, Colorado. That summer, with a bulldozer and crew, Jensen excavated lots of bones. The most remarkable was found late in the summer by Jim's son Ron. Ron was digging by himself a few hundred yards from camp when he uncovered a dinosaur **scapula,** or shoulder blade. This was no ordinary shoulder blade. As Ron chipped away the rock, he saw that the bone was very long—nearly eight feet long! Dinosaur Jim's own shoulder blade is only half a foot long, and Dinosaur Jim is well over six feet tall. This shoulder blade was almost 15 times as long as his own. So Dinosaur Jim knew right away that he was looking at part of an enormous dinosaur.

Opposite page: A paleontologist sketches the huge pelvic bone of a dinosaur in Dry Mesa Quarry. Many more fossils remain in Dry Mesa (left), some of which could be bigger than any known dinosaurs.

Comparing this bone to the shoulder blade of *Brachiosaurus* and other big sauropods, Jim Jensen figured that this dinosaur was larger than any known. It was probably longer than *Brachiosaurus*. Jensen called this giant *Supersaurus*. Further fossil discoveries indicate that *Supersaurus*'s bones resemble those of a diplodocid, one of those very long-tailed sauropods. Stretching out its whiplike tail, this dinosaur might have been well over 100 feet long! Paleontologists came to this conclusion by checking the size of the bones that have been found and comparing them to more complete skeletons of other dinosaurs.

Seven years after he identified *Supersaurus,* Dinosaur Jim Jensen was digging in the same Dry Mesa quarry when he found another shoulder blade, even bigger than *Supersaurus*'s. This bone was nearly 9 feet long, and far wider than the bone

from *Supersaurus*. Jensen figured this bone belonged to a brachiosaur-type sauropod. Given the width and thickness of the bone, this dinosaur was probably much heavier than *Supersaurus*. Both these giants lived and died in the same place 145 million years ago, though they may not have lived side by side. Perhaps this dinosaur died years earlier than *Supersaurus* and washed into the same ancient stream bed. There, sand covered over both dinosaurs. The sand then turned into rock over hundreds of years, preserving parts of both dinosaurs as fossils.

Dinosaur Jim named this new-found giant *Ultrasaurus.* *Ultra* means "the most," and Dinosaur Jim chose the name thinking that this dinosaur was the heaviest and perhaps the longest of all. He figured this dinosaur would have weighed more than 50 tons, measured nearly 100 feet long, and stood more than 6 stories tall. Because brachiosaur-like dinosaurs were more solidly built than diplodocid dinosaurs, Jensen's *Ultrasaurus* may have been the biggest dinosaur of them all according to weight.

But because *Ultrasaurus* is known from just a few bones, other dinosaur scientists aren't sure it is truly a different species. Perhaps it is just a very large *Brachiosaurus.* Nor do they know exactly how long or heavy it might have been. But it certainly was an enormous animal.

Was there ever a longer dinosaur than *Supersaurus* and *Ultrasaurus?* Yes. We now know of at least one. The title of longest dinosaur was taken in 1991, though the discovery of this giant was made in 1979.

A model of *Brachiosaurus.* Because so few *Ultrasaurus* fossils have been found, some scientists believe it is just an especially large *Brachiosaurus.*

The hikers who found the remains of the longest dinosaur were looking for these petroglyphs, ancient writings carved in rock, near Zia, New Mexico.

On a hot New Mexico day that year, backpackers Jan Cummings and Arthur Loy were walking along the side of a rocky mesa in the desert. They came across some gigantic bones sticking out of the rock wall. The hikers were on government land and knew not to take the bones. Valuable scientific information can be lost and fossils damaged when amateurs remove them without a scientist's guidance. Besides, the bones belonged to the government. So the hikers wisely took pictures of the fossils. But the site was not explored fully until 1985, when they showed the photos to Dr. David Gillette, who was then a paleontologist at the New Mexico Museum of Natural History in Albuquerque.

Models mark the place where the hikers found the huge dinosaur vertebrae.

In 1985, Dr. Gillette organized a dig at the site of these giant bones. In a single weekend, he and ten helpers dug out eight huge vertebrae, still lined up as they had been on a single living dinosaur nearly 150 million years ago. Dr. Gillette's crew hoped that much more of the dinosaur remained there, buried deep in the sandstone of the hill.

Over the next several summers, Dr. Gillette and his crew labored hard to **excavate,** or dig out, the bones of the giant.

They did so the old-fashioned way, which paleontologists around the world still use. They dug away the rock over the fossil. Then, when they got close to the layer of bone, they began carefully chipping away the rock with small tools—chisels and awls. When bones appeared, they carefully dug around them, put plaster over bone surfaces and surrounding rock, and then removed the bones and rock in huge plaster casts.

But Dr. Gillette also experimented with new methods to find the hidden bones. With scientists from the United States government's nearby Sandia and Los Alamos Laboratories, and Oak Ridge National Laboratory in Tennessee, he and his team tried looking for bones with many gadgets. They used gamma ray detectors, machines that click loudly when they detect radioactive materials such as uranium in the ground. Over millions of years, uranium has seeped into many dinosaur bones as they became fossils.

Dr. Gillette and his team also looked for dinosaur bones with sound detectors, like the sonar used to look for ships in the sea. By bouncing sounds beneath the ground, these machines could detect the pattern made when the sounds bounced off objects. Perhaps bones could be blocking the sound waves. But rocks could do the same, so the signals didn't necessarily mean that bones were present.

Members of Dr. Gillette's crew putting plaster on the bones of the huge dinosaur before excavating them

Scientists from Los Alamos National Laboratory using ground-penetrating sound detectors to search for dinosaur bones.

Dr. Gillette and his crew also used ultraviolet lights to search for bones, because many fossils glow under this kind of light. Fossil collectors have found glowing dinosaur bones when they shone their ultraviolet lights into uranium mines. That's because a mineral called hydroxyapatite found in all living bones and in well-preserved fossils makes them glow under ultraviolet light.

None of these new methods has yet proved to be a surefire way to find bones. But using these and more traditional methods, Dr. Gillette did manage to extract most of the body of a dinosaur from the New Mexico site.

Even before these bones were out of the ground, Dr. Gillette realized he had uncovered a truly enormous sauropod dinosaur. He knew it was a sauropod because the huge backbones had tall, straight spines, a shape and size found only among these giant plant-eating dinosaurs. He began measuring the huge bones to determine just how big the animal might have been. The bones were so big that Dr. Gillette even used a new measurement, "elephant units," to describe the animal's size, for it was clearly bigger than a dozen bull elephants.

Judging by the tail bones, Dr. Gillette estimates that this dinosaur was well over 100 feet long, perhaps even 150 feet. He made this estimate by comparing the tail bones to those of a nearly complete skeleton of the sauropod *Diplodocus*. *Diplodocus*'s bones were far shorter than the new dinosaur's, and the animal measured little more than half as long. He made measurements of *Diplodocus* skeletons in several museums, since this dinosaur was similar in the build of its backbones to the new dinosaur. The new dinosaur's bones were about 10 to 50 percent bigger than those of *Diplodocus*. So Dr. Gillette figured the new dinosaur must be at least 20 feet longer than *Diplodocus*, which measured 80 feet or longer. That length estimate made Dr. Gillette's new dinosaur by far the longest dinosaur known—possibly half a football field in length.

Dr. David Gillette

After years of careful study, Dr. Gillette scientifically described and named the dinosaur in 1991. He named the dinosaur *Seismosaurus hallorum*. *Seismosaurus* means "Earth-shaker reptile." The species name, *hallorum,* was for Reverend James Hall, director of the Ghost Ranch Conference Center, a fossil-rich museum in New Mexico, and Ruth Hall, Dr. Hall's fossil-collecting wife.

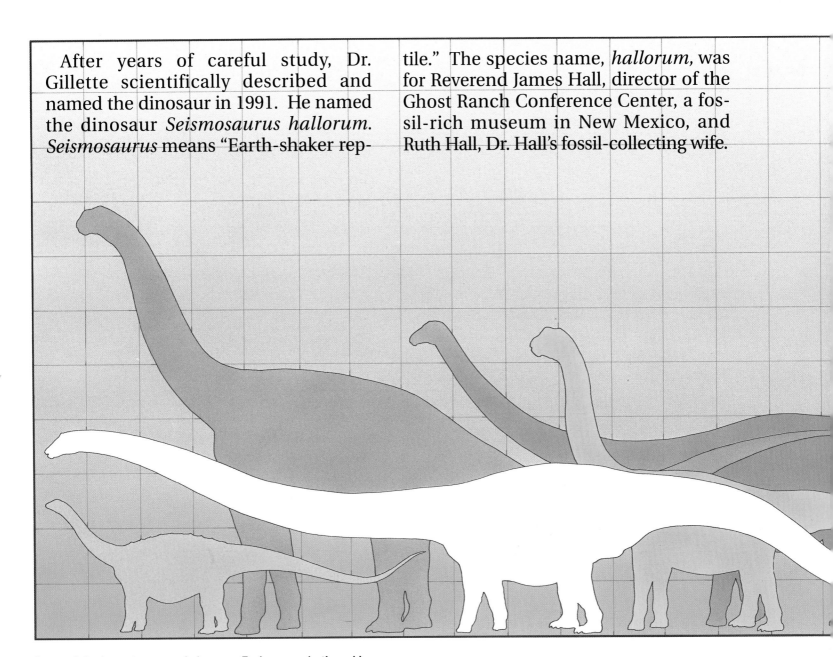

Some of the largest sauropods known. Each square in the grid represents five feet.

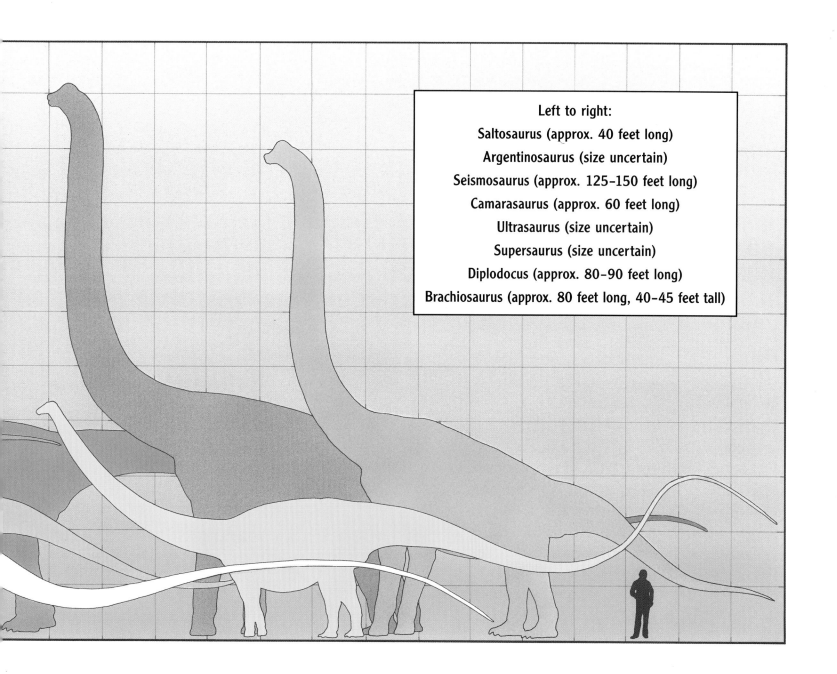

Left to right:
Saltosaurus (approx. 40 feet long)
Argentinosaurus (size uncertain)
Seismosaurus (approx. 125–150 feet long)
Camarasaurus (approx. 60 feet long)
Ultrasaurus (size uncertain)
Supersaurus (size uncertain)
Diplodocus (approx. 80–90 feet long)
Brachiosaurus (approx. 80 feet long, 40–45 feet tall)

Dr. Gillette and other scientists think that *Seismosaurus* was a diplodocid, with a long tail and short limbs. The long tail-bones and straight-up spines on *Seismosaurus's* backbones identify it as a member of the diplodocid family. But it is longer and stockier than other members of this sauropod group. It was different enough in shape, not to mention size, for Dr. Gillette to decide it was a new species of dinosaur—one he named *Seismosaurus*. That identification is much more certain than Dinosaur Jim Jensen's naming of *Ultrasaurus,* which is known from far fewer bones, with less distinctive features.

Dr. Gillette and his colleagues learned more about *Seismosaurus* than just its appearance. They also discovered how it lived, and perhaps how it died. Dr. Gillette found *Seismosaurus's* bones in what had been a stream channel more than 145 million years ago. Ancient streambeds, now turned to sandstone rocks, are good places to find fossil skeletons. Animals that die near or in the stream can be covered over quickly with sand and kept from rotting away in the open air. Over a great many years, their bones can turn to fossils as minerals enter into the spaces in the bone.

grind up the food in their guts. Scientists believe that sauropod dinosaurs swallowed rocks to help them digest. After all, these giants had skulls only as big as horse's heads on bodies as big as buildings. Their teeth were small and pencil-shaped, and could not grind huge quantities of food. So they must have just clipped plants with their teeth and done most of their digesting in their giant stomach vats.

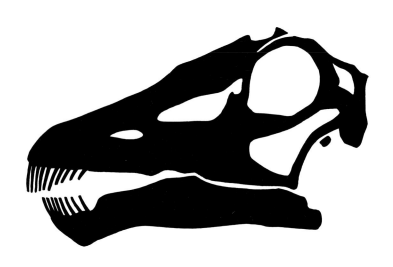

A *Diplodocus* skull, showing the small, narrow teeth that most sauropods had

Dr. Gillette didn't just find fossils at the *Seismosaurus* site. He and his crew also found about a bucket worth of rocks. These were very distinctive rocks, not like the ones usually found in that area. Except for one grapefruit-sized rock, all of these rocks were smaller than a tennis ball. And many were smooth and waxy.

Dr. Gillette realized that these rocks were **gastroliths,** or stomach stones. Many birds today, including chickens, swallow little pieces of grit to help them

The largest and smallest gastroliths found near the *Seismosaurus* skeleton

To help digest the food, some sauropod dinosaurs swallowed rocks and carried them long distances in their stomachs as they traveled in search of plants to eat. Inside a chamber of their stomachs, the stones mixed with stomach acid to break up plants into a pulp that was easy to digest.

Gastroliths had been discovered before, but never in such numbers. These stones show not only how *Seismosaurus* lived, but also how it may have died. The one very large stone found near the body of *Seismosaurus* might be an oversized rock that the dinosaur swallowed by mistake. The dinosaur may have choked or suffered a stomach blockage from the oversized rock.

A collection of dinosaur gastroliths

Imagine, then, that the ground-shaker has thumped its way to the stream with a choking pain. It bends its long neck to drink from the stream, hoping to move the big stone that is making it so uncomfortable. But it is too late, and the sick dinosaur collapses into the stream. Scavengers may come and pick at the body, but soon, the flowing sand on the stream bottom covers over the skeleton.

The longest dinosaur of them all is hidden beneath rising layers of sand that harden into rock. Millions of years later, when this land has turned to desert, wind blows away the crumbling sandy rock and exposes a piece of the giant.

Dr. Gillette has moved on to Utah, where he is state paleontologist. But he still returns to New Mexico to study *Seismosaurus* and to work on its bones. Over several summers, Dr. Gillette and his crew have dug up 4 neck vertebrae, 8 back vertebrae and several ribs, several linked tail vertebrae, and 20 others. The bend in some of the vertebrae that come from the beginning of the tail suggests that this section of the tail may have curved down. The rest of the tail, including its whip-like tip, was carried horizontally.

Perhaps one day an entire *Seismosaurus* can be found and mounted in a museum hall—a very large museum hall. Then the world will see the longest dinosaur in all its glory. The Earth Shaker will stand again.

And, probably, there are still longer, heavier giants in the ground, waiting to be found. Underneath the bleachers at the football stadium at Brigham Young University are dozens of huge fossils, in plaster jackets, some without labels. These are among the hundreds of huge bones that Jim Jensen dug at Dry Mesa and other quarries in Utah—so many bones that he didn't have time to identify and prepare them all. Perhaps even inside one of those plaster coverings lie new clues to which dinosaur was the longest of them all.

Pronunciation guide:

Argentinosaurus (ar-gen-teen-uh-SAW-rus)
Brachiosaurus (brak-ee-oh-SAW-rus)
carnivores (KAR-nuh-vorz)
Cretaceous (krih-TAY-shus)
Diplodocus (dih-PLOD-uh-kus)
excavate (EK-skuh-vait)
gastroliths (GAS-truh-lithz)
herbivorous (er-BIH-vuh-rus)
hydroxyapatite (hy-DROK-see-AH-puh-tyt)
paleontologists (pay-lee-on-TAHL-uh-jists)
sauropods (SAW-ruh-podz)
scapula (SKA-pyuh-luh)
Seismosaurus (syz-muh-SAW-ruhs)
titanosaurs (ty-TAN-uh-sorz)
vertebrae (VUR-tuh-bray)

Glossary

brachiosaurs: a group of huge, heavy sauropods

carnivores: animals that live on a diet of meat

Cretaceous: the last period during which dinosaurs lived, beginning 144 million years ago and lasting until 65 million years ago

diplodocids: a group of long, lightly built sauropods

fossils: the remains of a formerly living thing or its parts, usually preserved in rock or soil

gastroliths: stones that some dinosaurs swallowed to help them grind up their food

herbivorous: living on a diet of plants

Jurassic: the middle dinosaur period, from 208 million years ago until 145 million years ago

paleontologists: scientists who study life forms from ancient times

predators: animals that hunt and kill other animals

sauropods: a group of plant-eating dinosaurs, many of which were very large

scapula: a bone in the shoulder, often called the shoulder blade

titanosaurs: a group of huge sauropods, some of which had armored sides

vertebrae: the bones that make up an animal's spine

Index

Photo Acknowledgments:

Photographs are reproduced through the courtesy of: © John D. Cunningham / Visuals Unlimited, pp. 8, 35; © François Gohier, pp. 11, 13, 20, 22; © A. J. Copley / Visuals Unlimited, p. 12; © Beth Davidow, pp. 18, 25, 26, 27, 29; John Weinstein/The Field Museum of Natural Science, neg. #6N86959.4 p. 19; George S. Eccles, Dinosaur Park, Ogden, UT, p. 24; © Dr. David Gillette, p. 34.